HOW TO FIX AMERICA

Restoring sanity and civility to
our Great Democracy in three simple steps

by Phillip A. Barlag

How to Fix America
© 2012 Phillip A. Barlag
All rights reserved.

ISBN-13:978-1479377534
ISBN-10:1479377538

To my wife Erin, the greatest person I know,
and to Ethan, Everett and Harper
and the world they will they inherit.

Disclaimer

The opinions contained in this book are solely those of the author, and do not represent any other individual or organization.

CONTENTS

INTRODUCTION
(please read)

I have written this brief book to explore how America can be great again. This is one person's idea on how to achieve everyone's ideal. America is a great nation, but deeply flawed and our political system has become unsustainable. It can no longer consistently provide the citizenry with good governance or policy. American politics has become a mob war, where each party is focusing solely on what the other is doing, watching their every move, and counter-attacking at every turn. The parties that are supposed to be setting policy are at war with each other, and the American people are casualties of the crossfire.

For the past few years, I've tried to swear off paying attention to politics. Like most people, I am fairly convinced that I am right most of the time. I also have a hard time owning up to being wrong. But lately I've come to terms with it. Being wrong is part of our nature and in trying to let go of my self-assured arrogance, I've realized that there are a lot of good ideas out there, and many of them come from people that I've spent a lot of time trying to prove wrong at my expense.

We're all wrong a lot. So are our elected officials. While most people can accept being wrong, those that lead our nation seem completely unable to do so. As a result, our elected officials move further apart, to increasingly extreme positions, and the system grinds to a halt. This crack in the foundation of the American political framework has dire consequences for the future of our system.

In writing this book, I have sought to be policy-neutral. I have tried not to judge any individual party or politician. I have not addressed a single social issue. Instead, I have chosen to focus on the structure of the system itself, and what I think can be done to address its fatal flaws. In other words, I have tried to make this the most apolitical book about politics ever.

This framework is not exhaustive. There are plenty of challenges that require attention and to address them all would easily extend this book by a factor of 1,000. My hope is that the framework for reform that I propose will address the timeless 80/20 rule: by making changes to 20% of the governance of the government, we can solve 80% of our challenges. In sharing these ideas with people in conversations, I'm often asked about the role of the media. After all, most of us access the government and its actions through the media. To me, to comment on the media would itself be a judgment of a social issue and thus undermine my quest for neutrality. Those opinions are outside the scope of this brief book.

While I am not a political scientist, I am qualified to write this book in one very important aspect: I am a citizen. The American government is my government. Its dysfunction impacts me, my family, my community and all my fellow citizens.

The world is not insular. America is part of a global economy. Americans are part of the human species. The policies of America and the effectiveness of its government directly or indirectly impact each of the more than 7 billion people on this planet. I believe that we have a moral obligation to set the tone for fair government and to understand that America is more meaningful than its national borders. Until we reform our government, we will continue to fail this moral obligation to ourselves and to the rest of the world.

I do not predict imminent doom. If the problem was so severe, we would be able to focus on solutions. The problem with America's decline is not that it is happening too quickly; it's that it's happening too slowly. If the problem was more acute, we could galvanize people behind a legitimate reform effort. But the system is atrophying slowly, gradually degrading. Slow decline makes it hard for anyone to pinpoint the problem and even harder to rally people to do anything in response. But I believe I have isolated the biggest problem.

Here's what I think we should do about it...

WHAT'S WRONG
WITH US?

Are you satisfied with the government you have?

I'm not. I want better. I deserve better. My family deserves better. My community deserves better. We all deserve better.

The American political system is in a state of high dysfunction. Acrimony and divisiveness are the defining characteristics of our policy-making institutions. It's pretty bad, but it could be worse. It's not exactly anarchy and the inertia in the system will keep the government in a state of decline for a long time; complete collapse will take decades or centuries.

History would suggest that collapse of complex political systems is the best way to bring about renewal. But for most Americans, the government has ceased to live up to its most basic promise: to serve the best interests of the American people. Waiting for the rotting edifice to come crumbling down just isn't good enough. There has to be a way to fix the problem without first witnessing its destruction.

There is. In fact, it's wonderfully simple.

But before we describe the solution, we must first define the problem. To me, the problem is clear: politics in America has become about nothing more than winning. American politics has become so full of hate and rancor that it has shifted from governance to a zero-sum game where the point is to hold power for its own sake. I think most people would agree that Washington, D.C. does not exactly exemplify civility. This is the root cause. Our system no longer rewards better policy positions, and doesn't really reflect how the American public wants policy-makers to act.

American politics now reflects nothing more than the endless cycle of winning and losing. Politics has become the ultimate team sport: people pick their side and root like hell. People send their representatives to Washington to beat the bad guys and elected officials are all too happy to play the part. These officials benefit the most because all they must do to retain power is criticize their opponents endlessly and rally the electorate to their banner. Fair-minded, balanced government is a thing of the past. The quality of legislation doesn't matter anymore.

If this sounds too simplistic, look deeper. How can such a political system represent the wildly diverse continuum of values represented by the American public? When the line is drawn in absolutes, there is no room for compromise. Imagine the power of drawing from the best of all ideologies to leverage the incredible diversity of this great nation. Instead, we have two extremist parties defined only by their myopia and drive to 'expose' their counterparts as evil, corrupt and subversive. The inevitable consequence is divisiveness. The efficacy of policy is fully subservient to the goal of power. As a result, policy stinks. We all lose.

If everything is about winning and losing, there is no room for rational discourse and informed policy. Instead of dealing with key issues, politicians simply appease a 'base' and pander to the people. Populism permeates every aspect of politics.

We make the best decisions when we are aligned to a higher purpose. Government used to be based on the noble ideal of doing what was best for the people. We need to restore this sense of higher purpose. We need to break the cycle of win/lose, where everyone loses. We need to push people together, drive politicians to the center and take a stick of dynamite to the wall at the party divide. To stop the terminal decline of our policy-making institutions, we need to force the spirit of cooperation and collaboration between our elected officials. We need to neuter the party system.

A friend of mine once called herself a 'crazy cat lady.' I once asked her how she got her existing cats and new ones to get along. Her solution was brilliant in its simplicity. She would rub the water from some canned tuna on the top of each of their heads, put them in a room together and wait. Eventually, despite their natural tendency to be wary of each other, the cats would give in and begin to lick the tuna off each other. In almost no time, bonds were forged and the animals lived in blissful coexistence. So how do we do this with our politicians? We must come to terms with the fact that they are no longer in it for us, only themselves. It's time to lock them in a room and force them to collaborate.

The diversity of opinions and experiences inside America is extraordinary. Think of all the talent and human capacity being wasted by all the petty squabbling. Our system divides people into segments and turns them against each other.

Rather than being able to draw from a wide pool of ideas and solutions, we lock people into silos and the country suffers.

As bad as things are, they are not so bad as to be unsolvable. Even better news: the system doesn't need to be torn down to be repaired. If the problem is that divisiveness is the root cause of our mediocre government, we can and must force politicians to work together, no matter what party they belong to. Only by bringing all parties to the table can we chart a path forward for our nation. Otherwise, the fault line that is the party divide will tear us to pieces.

We know what we can't do: blow up the system and start from scratch. We know what we must do: restore sanity and civility to our policy-making institutions and the people that lead them. In the next chapter, we will take a good, hard look at what we're trying to restore. Then, we will show how to do it.

What's wrong with us?

What's wrong with us?

(Some of)
WHAT MAKES
AMERICA GREAT

(Some of)
WHAT MAKES
AMERICA GREAT

As dire as things may seem, every generation in American history has predicted the imminent collapse of the political order. But rather than catastrophe, the result is usually so much more decline. The arc of history follows a trend line. Through the lens of history, our current political situation is no different than other periods in our past. But there is one crucial difference: we have lost our ability to cope with differences of opinion. Our system is completely paralyzed by a never-ending cycle of vitriol and recrimination. There is no time where we admit the other side has a point and chart a path forward together.

Still, no matter how unproductive our system has become, there are many things that make America great. Any analysis of what changes have to be made to repair broken institutions should consider why striving for change is worth the effort in the first place. Let's take a moment and explore some of the ways that America is great, and where we've lost touch.

There is no way this can be exhaustive. America is great in so many ways that a full inventory of this country's strengths would span multiple volumes. But in defining the challenges we face as a civil society, it's important to cover a few characteristics of American greatness, and where they are being subverted by our political process. In the interest brevity, this section will drill in on a just few key topics but please be assured that there are more than just a few things right with America.

Debate, compromise and diversity

Debate and compromise are cornerstones of this great country. No one person or party has all the answers. No one framework for the establishment of policy is superior to any other. America is at its best when we draw from the widest pool of ideas and set policy based on what is best for the country, not whose power is consolidated. Political impasse happens when there is no consensus between those in power. Such moments are a unique window, a gift. They allow our policy makers to explore new ideas and find a compromise position. By its very definition, a compromise is a centrist position. This is a hedge against extremism. In American history, the times of greatest strife have come when some portion of the population was trying to wrest power away from a group holding steadfast to an extremist position. The times of greatest breakthrough have come when key stakeholders came to the negotiating table with an open mind as the only table stakes required to play.

We don't have debate; we have class warfare. Not class in an economic sense, but in a political sense. Instead of dialog we have empty rhetoric. We don't have compromise; we have a contest of wills. One party fights like hell to block the success of the other while in the minority, and then rushes to push through as much of its agenda as it can when in the majority, before it runs out of political capital. Policy has become an all-or-nothing game and there is a no-man's land in the middle. The center is a ghost town.

We have lost our structural capacity to compromise, and the very rare examples of centrism are usually held against the parties. It has been suggested that compromise only waters down policy. This is utter nonsense. The Constitution is only evidence that needs to be submitted.

"We the people of the United States, in order to form a more perfect union…" A more perfect union. Beautiful. The union can be improved; it needs to be better. What a wonderful sentiment. The Founders never settled for the status quo. When the system was broken, they sought to fix it. The transition from "The United States in Congress Assembled" as organized by the Articles of Confederation to "The United States of America" as defined by the Constitution took a lot of blood, sweat and tears. And more than anything else, it took a lot of compromise.

History views the Constitution with an extraordinary amount of nostalgia. It is, after all, the foundation upon which our entire country is built. Political battles have been fought with alarming frequency about which party is more 'true' to the Constitution. But by even arguing on such grounds, everyone loses. The Constitution was never a zero-sum game, where one party got everything they demanded and the other got nothing. No one 'won' in the framing of the Constitution. The document took shape when all of the delegates to the Constitutional Convention put forth their requirements, debated on the points of conflict, and crafted a framework that to this day is held up as the perfect embodiment of governance – and of compromise. Some delegates refused to sign, and went home to prepare to have the document defeated, but the majority agreed that their combined efforts had produced the best overall result. This country was founded on a spirit of compromise. Without this spirit we would never have had the Constitution and without the Constitution, we would not be the greatest country on Earth.

That said, there are some systemic flaws in the Constitution. It was a great document for framing governance, but it didn't do the best job of ensuring equality. As the country has evolved, participation in the system has expanded to include previously excluded peoples. We are a stronger nation for it.

America is a nation of diversity like none other. Our citizenry is drawn from almost every nation, culture and heritage. We must embrace the diversity to lead this country forward. The bigger the pool of ideas and perspectives from which to create policy, the better policy will be. Further, greater access to the political system from all people will lead to greater diversity in the political gene pool. Our record on diversity has been mixed in our history. In general, we're heading in the right direction in terms of creating an equalitarian society, but falling far short in translating this to our political institutions. How can America realize its full potential if we don't fully tap into the enormous human potential offered by its collective citizenry?

One of the most powerful features of our Democracy is the ability to make each other more well-informed. Our views are supposed to change, evolve, adapt. Governing a country as complex as the United States is overwhelmingly complex. There's no way any one person or group of people can get it all right. There's no such thing as 'all right' in the first place.

One of the premises in this book is that we are all wrong a lot. Being wrong is part of being human. Most of us have no problem owning up to not being omniscient. Our politicians, however, cannot seem to admit mistakes or changes of position. They're too dug in.

America is like a tarnished piece of Paul Revere silver: full of history and meaning, but very much needing a good polish to restore its shine and luster.

A DISTRIBUTION OF POLITICAL IDEOLOGY: A BRIEF DETOUR THROUGH STATISTICS

One of the underlying assumptions that this book makes is that political ideology is a continuum. If it could be statistically quantified, political ideology would resemble a normal distribution under a bell curve. In this metaphor, the mean – or center point of the population – would be the truly centrist political position. To the right of the curve is the Republican point of view, which grows increasingly conservative as it moves further away from the mean. To the left of the mean is the Democratic point of view, which grows increasingly liberal is it moves further away from the mean.

In a normal distribution, 68 percent of the population is plus or minus one standard deviation away from the mean. (Please note, I only choose left and right because that is the language we use to describe these parties. Do not read into the corresponding plus and minus as an implication of right and wrong.) I would contend that this is absolutely true of politics in America. Most people can reasonably agree on most things. Someone who is one standard deviation to the right of the mean has a lot in common with someone who is one standard deviation to the left of the mean. In fact, these people often have more in common and agree in general terms with the extremists from within their own parties. The problem is that our system does not allow these people to work with and inform each other. There is a big, brick wall right in the middle and most people cannot get through or around this divide.

The divide is, of course, the party line. Returning to a metaphor used earlier, this is a no-man's land that sits between the trench warfare of party politics. To venture to cross it amounts to a suicide charge: possibly courageous, almost always fruitless. Our centrist politicians lie dead on the field of battle, whether from enemy fire, or a bullet in the back from the more extreme elements of their own party. We need to blow apart the down the wall at the middle and allow for the true majority to rise – the moderate majority.

We could argue the appropriateness of using a normal distribution to make a point about political ideology. After all, it is probably simplistic to suggest that ideas can be translated to points on a statistical chart. But I believe the example is extremely informative to the current state of politics in America, if not literally, then metaphorically.

So far we have looked at the problems we face, some of what makes America great and a framework through which to view moderate government. Now let's look at a system that will unlock true reform and restore civility to our great Democracy.

STEP ONE:
THE PRESIDENCY

Our next presidential election will be the last in our history. We will vote for a president to serve one, six-year term. Not much has changed so far. But here's where it gets good. After the presidential election, we hold a second general election – for Vice President. The Vice President will be the candidate the American people best feel offers balance to the President. The Vice President will always be of the opposite party of the President. If a Democrat is President, A Republican will be Vice President and vice versa.

At the end of the six-year term in office, the President steps down and is succeeded by the Vice President. This brings the opposite party into power. But as you can see, it's not indefinite. Every six years, another election will be held and the new Vice President is elected from the opposite party. Crucial to this process is the opening up of the vote to all Americans. All VP candidates are voted into office by all Americans. By having Americans choose from the best candidate from one party at a time, these candidates must be centrist, moderate, and have appeal to the full range of political spectrum in America.

But the VP must be more than a President-in-waiting. The VP must be a partner. This is on the job training at its finest. What better way than to prepare to be the leader of the free world than to know the job is yours in a few short years, and learn up-close how the office of the President functions? The President and the VP will work together on policy by having the VP participate in the Cabinet and by serving as a Presidential Advisor. There is no need for the VP to set himself up as a vocal opposition critic; the VP is now a partner in power and their legacies are now tied together. By bringing the President and Vice President together for policy decisions, they are each enriched with greater depth of ideology and perspectives. All of America is better represented for the balance they create.

As the senior magistrate, the President still has his traditional role as head of state. This will not and should not change. Executive decisions still rest with the President.

Once we have established the practice of creating equilibrium and civility in the office of the President, the rest falls into place.

STEP TWO:
THE HOUSE OF
REPRESENTATIVES

The goal of these reforms is to re-establish the political center of gravity and open our system back up to the best of everyone. The House of Representatives will serve to further bring balance to the new political order and put Representatives back in touch with the people they are intended to represent.

Leadership and Majority

Whichever party has the President in office, the alternate party will now comprise the House leadership, regardless of actual majority. All committee chairs and the Speaker will thus serve as an effective counter-weight to the White House. Not an obstacle, but a check.

Today, the opposition party does little more than try to stop all legislation from the other party. We've gone from governance to guerilla warfare. With the Presidential reforms in place, the House of Representatives now has no incentive to be obstructionist. The access to power is predictable and stable, like an economic price mechanism.

Calmer waters and cooler heads prevail. No one ideology can hijack the agenda.

What does increase is the need for civility and compromise. The opposition party must work with the President. In just a few short years, the opposition will gain the Presidency. If they want their policies to have a voice, they will have to be cooperative responsible for the House leadership. The shoe will be on the other foot pretty soon.

In addition to tying the fate of the President and the House of Representative to one another, the consequences of gaining and holding Congressional majorities shrinks precipitously. The criticality of winning every seat vanishes, and those in the House can do what they are really supposed to do: serve their constituency.

In order to be effective representatives of my political values, they have to know who I am. I would love to know my Congressmen. I have lived in countless Congressional districts – represented by people from both major parties. I have never met one of my Congressmen. I have never shaken hands with or looked in the eye of the person who is supposed to typify and defend my point of view in the Federal Government.

I have, however, gotten lots and lots of fund-raising phone calls. I have gotten lots of emails. I have gotten newsletters. My relationship with my Congressmen has always been one-way, despite my occasional attempts to the contrary.

I have long held a fantasy of running a simple social experiment that would start with finding one participant from every single Congressional district. At the same time and on the same day, have each one begin a standard process by which they attempt to have a live conversation with their elected representative. At every step of the way, track the progress. Every phone call, every request for a meeting, every polite dismissal from a staffer, every successful conversation, every single outreach, all of it would be codified. I can only imagine the fun a statistician could have with such a data set.

I've never run the experiment for two reasons. First, I don't know that many people willing to indulge my absurdity, and second, because I don't need to. No comprehensive study is needed to validate what we all know: It's obvious that Congress is out of touch. There is no need to quantify how out of touch it is; it doesn't matter.

If the path to the White House was predictable and stable, then the House of Representatives would be much more effective. Not only would they have to cease trying to undermine the President so that they increase their chances of having their own party in power, but they also would be free to look outside the Beltway and better serve their districts. Rather than firing away on the front lines of the war on reason that defines our current Congressional set-up, Representatives could instead invest their time getting to know their constituents and bringing those perspectives back to Washington. They would also be liberated to hear what all their constituents think, not just those belonging to their political party. After all, isn't a Representative supposed to represent everyone from their districts, and not just the ones that share a party affiliation?

This is critical because there is no person in the Federal government that is supposed to have a greater intimacy with their constituency than a Congressional Representative.

Intimacy enables trust and understanding, and this is a process that unfolds over time, not achieved by a flip of the light switch. Trust is earned, not given. The two sides need to get to know each other. Congressional Representatives and their constituents are like a married couple that needs a long weekend away without the kids to rekindle their love for each other.

Term limits in the House of Representatives

A term limit system must consider the nature of the intimate relationship between constituents and Representatives. While term limits are both important and necessary to ensure a transition to a moderate government, over-reaching would carry its own set of undesirable consequences. In other words, there has to be a limit to term limits.

Accordingly, the system will establish term limits in the House of Representatives at ten terms. Ten two-year terms is 20 years. 20 years is plenty of time to develop a trusted and intimate relationship with a constituency. But it's also just enough without being too much. 20 years is a generation and a full generation is plenty of time to serve a community. It's also the right time to step aside and give someone else a chance.

Values change over time. Just think of the difference between America in 1940, 1960, 1980, 2000, etc. As values change, so too must the people who are tasked with representing those values. In addition, the American system needs a greater distribution of access to power, creating space for new voices and new values.

Of course, a ten-term limit doesn't guarantee ten terms. Those in Congress must stand for re-election and have their work voted on as always. However, once Congress is returned to a sense of sanity and civility, the quality of the service provided by the Representatives will improve. Constituents will be happier as their viewpoints are more fully articulated in the mechanics of government.

As the system is at a more stable center of gravity, there is no need to alter the current method of electing someone to Congress. The current electoral process works fine.

Leadership in the House

Where the process must change is what happens once the elected get to Washington, D.C. The real issue with term limits comes into play with committee chairmanships. Holding committee chairmanships year over year, term over term, decade over decade collapses power into the hands of a few. There is nothing Democratic about this. America is a country of the people, for the people and by the people. Creating such exclusive access to such extraordinary power is fundamentally at odds with the American ideal.

So while Congressional term limits are set at ten terms, the issue of committee chairs is different. There must be a cap. It will be three terms atop any committee.

The ranking member of the minority party must work with the chairman in a similar way to how the VP must sit side by side with the President. At the six-year change in control, this individual, provided they are still in office, will assume the chairmanship and the cycle renews itself. This is a consequence of the change in party leadership every six years. Where the cap really comes into play is what happens when the leadership reverts back after a six-year interlude. In theory, a Representative could be a committee chair, step aside at the six-year change in leadership, and still be in office when the next cycle comes about. In our new system, Representatives can serve only once as a committee chair. No more power collapsing into the hands of a few. No more using committee positions as a weapon in the war for power. When the six-year change in leadership happens, the slate is wiped clean and the next generation of leaders steps in. The House exists to serve the people. It did once and it will again.

STEP THREE:
THE SENATE

This chapter on the Senate is the shortest of the three steps. Once the Presidency and the House of Representatives have been addressed to create balance and predictability, the Senate is easy. The Senate is intended to be an august body, full of the most experienced policy-makers in the country. With two from each state, the Senate ensures that even little states can have a big voice. The votes representing the least populous state count every bit as much as those from the most populous.

There is something wonderful in that Wyoming, our least populous state, has two Senators but – because each state's delegation to the House of Representatives is established by population – only one Representative. California by contrast, has two Senators, but 53 Representatives.

When viewed from a national perspective – 50 States, two Senators each, 100 total Senators. Clean and simple. Except, it's not 100 Senators as one body. No, the Senate is really two groups of Senators – the representatives from each party – that combine to 100. Sometimes the distribution is close, other times it's skewed toward one party or the other. The party distribution in the Senate ebbs and flows over time. But no matter what, for the American public, it's yet another field of battle in the endless party warfare. Great laws go to die in the Senate and bad ones are born there. The American public is, yet again, underserved by those elected to be their voice.

The fix is simple: restore the balance. Each state sends two Senators to Washington, D.C. and these two must be drawn from both parties. One Democrat, one Republican. There is no majority, there is no minority; there is only balance.

With this balance, the Senate will much more effectively carry out its responsibilities. For example, there is no need to defeat or stall good appointees to federal office on party grounds; confirmation can now be solely determined by merit and fit.

As with the House of Representatives, developing a relationship with a constituency is an important function of a Senator. As with the President and with Representatives, Senators will step aside to allow for others to serve. Two, six-year terms is enough time to be of service, and to create room for more participation in the political process.

Our Constitution was amended to limit a President to two terms largely to ensure that no one person had too much power. This same principle must apply in other bodies of the government. Term limits create access for more people to participate in the administration of government. They also allow for policy to be set by a diverse group of people, bringing fresh ideas and perspectives to the table. The more diversity of thought within the government, the better the system will be. As with the other branches of government, the Senate must be gradually reconstituted over time to enable greater access to the political system and to reflect the ever-shifting values of the populace.

Leadership positions in the Senate and its committees are distributed equally. No Senator can serve more than one term as a committee chair. The Senate needs to refresh itself. There is too much power consolidated in the hands of too few. This is completely contradictory to the spirit of American governance. It's not what was intended and it's not what we deserve.

As an aside, you may have noticed that I have not mentioned the judiciary. The challenges facing the judiciary are much more complex than outflows of partisan politics. If we follow the 80/20 rule, rooting out the issues within the judiciary is an enormously complex challenge that yields only incremental benefit, when compared against the benefits of fixing the broader political system.

With the power structure stabilized and predictable, there will be no incentive for any justices to pay loyalty to any political party. Personally, I believe the idea of 'judicial activism' is greatly overstated, and that, by and large, our justices are reasonable, informed and fair. But to whatever extent this is not true, over time, the judiciary will come to even more fully exemplify these virtues. As our elected officials learn to play nice with each other, and govern as opposed to seek power, the candidates they will nominate to the judiciary will be all the better.

Summary:

Step 1: Presidents serve for six year terms. They are always succeeded by their sitting Vice President, who represents the opposition party and is elected by a general election. There are no more Presidential elections.

Step 2: Establish term limits of ten terms for the House of Representatives and a three-term and one leadership cycle limit on serving as chairman of any committee. Leadership in the House is determined by which party sits in opposition to the President's party, and majority no longer matters.

Step 3: Each state appoints one Senator from each party. Senators have two-term limits and can only serve as a committee chair for one, six-year term.

Holding political office is no longer a proxy for power. Under this new system, politics is a means to serve the American people. We will force those in Washington to serve our interest, not theirs.

UNITY AND PURPOSE

When rallied together with a sense of common purpose, the American people can do amazing things. December 7, 1941 may be a date that will live in infamy, but December 8, 1941 and the days and years that followed showed the world what America can do when united. The horror of the September 11, 2001 terror attacks also awoke in Americans a long-dormant sense of national pride. When united, America can do amazing things.

No one party typifies right and no one party typifies wrong. Any intimation that people belonging to one party or the other is more prone to goodness or corruption is just stupid. No one is more or less good or bad because of party affiliation.

Under this system, politics shifts from the extreme political poles, to the center. Everyone votes for everyone. Moderation rules the day. We're all in it together and we'll drag our elected officials along with us. We can be greatly united like those exceptional times in our history. We shouldn't need to have a horribly national tragedy to bring our country together. We can and will unite, and will force our elected officials to do the same.

Imagine having the best of both parties. What a wonderful

idea. We can get there and we don't have to completely deconstruct the system. This is minor innovation, not a revolution. The only destruction is to the wall in the middle.

Together, we can enjoy a better America.

The beauty of this system is that it creates predictability. Economists talk about the need to have price predictability in order to make investment decisions. Politics is no different. When the predictability of power is guaranteed, it is safe to walk the middle ground.

This changes nothing about the fundamental nature of the structure of the American ideal. Well, that's not exactly true: it enhances the American ideal. The political agenda can no longer be hijacked by extremists. Everyone's point of view matters, even the extremists themselves. The only difference is that there is no difference anymore. We have ceased to define our political system by concrete walls and instead have changed to a continuum. A bell curve, where the mean is the true center of political ideology, and the majority of people are plus or minus one standard deviation from the mean.

IMPLEMENTATION

One of the core premises of this framework is that there is no need to blow up the American system of governance in order to fix it. In fact, minor innovations can yield the greatest impact because they build on core strengths. The beauty of the American system is that there are still – despite all its flaws – many core strengths upon which to build. Rather than being radical this framework is inherently conservative. Maybe a better phrase would be mild-mannered.

There is only so much change that institutions can handle at once. In order to be most effective, this system is one that should be phased-in over time. The mechanism by which this is accomplished is through the term-limits of Presidents, Representatives and Senators.

Phasing in term limits for the Presidency is easy enough. It will only take one Presidential / Vice Presidential election cycle before the system achieves equilibrium in the Oval Office. The next Presidential election is our last. What a wonderful thought. Six years later and the transition of power will be smooth, predictable and, hopefully, dull. There is no need for a long-term phase-in of the modification to the Presidential system. Anyone eligible for election now would be eligible for election to the six-year term. In theory this means that a President could serve a four-year term and before their term of office expires, the system is enacted. At this point, they run for office in the final Presidential election, win, and serve their six-year term. By pressing the 'reset' button, one President could, in theory, serve for ten years. While this exceeds the current cap of eight years, under this system, the latter six years will be more productive, balanced and representative of the will of the people. This is a positive trade-off for the extra two years in office. Besides, it only happens once. From there its six years and done.

Term limits for the Senate are a little trickier, but only marginally. By the time the 2012 election cycle comes around, nearly 40 Senators would be over their term limit (www.senate.gov). A 40% turnover in one cycle is too radical. Once the changes to the system take place, our elected officials will have incentive to work with each other more cohesively, and not be prohibited by crossing the no-man's land of the party divide. Thus, the urgency to immediately remove elected officials from office is someone what abated.

Of course, some turnover will be accomplished through natural attrition. Not every Senator is elected in perpetuity and not all serve for decades like Strom Thurman (48 years) or Robert Byrd (51 years). But for those that have already served two terms, term limits will be phased-in according to seniority: the longer the service, the faster the phase-out out. Within 12 years, all Senators that have already served two terms must be phased out. By accomplishing the phase-out gradually, the system will absorb the change seamlessly, allowing for a smooth transfer of power. The positive knowledge accumulated over the years – how to govern the country – can be passed on to the next generation of leadership. The negative and destructive knowledge – how to consolidate power for its own sake – will be useless and irrelevant.

The House of Representatives is another story entirely. Any representative who has already served ten or more terms will no longer be eligible to stand for election. One quick slice of the knife and a new generation of leadership is born. With every election cycle there will be a new crop of Representatives no longer eligible to stand for reelection. In just a few years, we will completely turn over Congressional leadership, allowing for more dynamic and adaptable policy, and greater modernization of the values reflected in our laws.

The end of electioneering

The extreme politics of our elected officials begins even before they are elected. When candidates seek election, they have to first be nominated by their party. In order to be nominated by their party, they have to make a case that they best represent the ideals of that party. This leads to a rush away from the center, with candidates using the inflammatory rhetoric of extreme politics to differentiate themselves, appeal to the radical elements of their parties and grab headlines. The media loves a sound bite and elections bring out the most extreme politics has to offer. Candidates seeking to identify themselves as the most 'true' to an idealized ideology are all too happy to oblige. A quick glance at any campaign ad in primary season will validate this idea.

But what happens once a candidate gets nominated? They are going into an election and running against someone of the opposite party. Assuming there is even the slightest bit of parity in the contest, the game is to try and steal as many votes from the other party as possible. Candidates now want to try and be as centrist as possible, to appeal to the broadest possible base. All things being equal, at least one candidate in an election needs to have some 'cross-over' appeal to have a chance to win.

But candidates can only go so far in their journey to the center. They are bound to the extremes by the gravity of those that supported their candidacy in the first place. Often those that support candidates with the most enthusiasm (i.e., money) in the primary / nomination process are those that hold the most extreme views. Candidates in a general election cycle must conduct a very difficult balancing act, managing the tension of the extreme elements of their party, with the desire to appeal to moderates of both parties.

Isn't this just utter nonsense? Shouldn't we be able to cast votes based on who candidates actually are, not just who they want us to think they are?

In a system where moderate politics rules, the extreme elements of each party are diminished in importance. It's not rhetoric that rules; it's what a candidate actually stands for.

By bringing harmony and civility to politics, the moderate majority regain their influence as the most important group to keep happy. If Democrats get to vote for the best Republican candidates, and Republicans get to vote for the best Democratic candidates, all seeking office must be able to draw the most votes from the other party in order to win. Extremist candidates and policy positions will carry no weight – all that matters is the qualification for office. What a wonderful thought – being able to choose the best candidate from a pool of good people, and not having to choose between the lesser of two evils.

This system will manifest itself in the death of the primary system as we know it. When candidates declare themselves for the Vice Presidency, they will be from only one party – as certified by that party's National Committee – and then be selected by ALL Americans. No more primary attack ads on TV? For that matter, no more attack ads of any kind on TV!

Ending divisiveness, being wrong and changing our minds to form better opinions

No one is more or less likely to be good or bad because of party affiliation or political beliefs. No party has the market cornered on ethics and integrity, and no party suffers from a disproportionate ratio of corruption and avarice.

I can be deeply convinced that I am right, and disagree with someone who is deeply convinced that they are right. So which one of us is right? Both? Neither? One or the other? It's a false question. Right and wrong is truly relative to the opinion of the individual, and like it or not, people are entitled to their opinions.

If you accept the premise that most Americans are dissatisfied with the performance of our elected officials, why are we not able to do anything about it? Are we stuck with this system forever? Do we have to watch as the lemmings in D.C. continue to run toward the cliff? Or can something be done?

America really must be rid of the crippling divisiveness

that is slowly ripping our great nation apart. It starts so early and it is ingrained as part of the political order. Our elected officials, and those that run for office against them, offer an illusion of knowing next to everything. This leads to extraordinary intransigence. Rather than allow points of view to adapt, ideologies become entrenched and frighteningly rigid. The no-man's land at the center of party politics grows more desolate and dangerous all the time. The consequence of this is severe. It means that we do not give our elected officials the capacity to grow and evolve their positions. Our politicians have been backed into a corner. Or more appropriately, they have all backed each other into a corner, and we keep them there.

The war of words is dispiriting, but the politics-as-war, kill or be kill mentality, masks a more frightening problem with our system – that we categorically refuse to allow elected officials to change their minds. After all, they've promised us that they already know everything; changing their mind is tantamount to saying 'I was wrong.' What self-respecting politician would admit to being wrong? The moment any elected official shifts party positions, they are hammered on all sides as being a flip-flopper. Instead of celebrating someone enlightened enough to suggest that they are not infallible, we criticize and condemn people for lacking the character to hold their positions. The media is all too complicit, poring over endless footage of speeches and press conferences in the attempt to catch politicians red-handed. Trying to fill space in a hyperactive, 24-hour news cycle the media seeks out and exploits anything that can be portrayed as contradiction.

Don't get me wrong, politicians shouldn't just say what the audience wants to hear in the moment. They need to actually stand for more than getting elected. Many of the instances of political contradiction are evidence of a candidate seeking political power for its own sake, and their willingness to attain office by any means. This is wholly different than someone evolving and adapting a position based upon growing, learning and adapting.

People have a lot to learn from people that disagree with them. If we are to progress as a society, and recapture our place as the leader of nations, we must have leaders that can adapt in a radically changing world. But if we are so unforgiving that as an electorate, we cannot embrace a leader who grows, we're in a lot of trouble. We need to allow for those that disagree with one another to bring a compendium of perspectives to the table in order to enrich policy. The alternative is what we have now, and that is clearly not working.

Hopefully by now, the case has been made that ideas need the ability to evolve. This can be carried forward to lead to better public policy. When the inputs are more flexible and open-minded, the resultant policy will be much better for all Americans. If we want a reasonable and moderate society, we need to a moderate and reasonable government. We will never have such a government until our elected officials both are, and are allowed to be, reasonable and moderate.

Until then, we will be stuck with what we have now, where our major policy frameworks tend to be driven by one 'side' or the other, depending on who is in power, and how much political capital they have to spend. Once that capital is exhausted, gridlock ensues until such time as one party can consolidate enough power to push through the next one-sided bill.

A much more effective approach would be to revive the old-fashioned compromise. Compromise requires contact. Fighting a war of words through the media, in an endless election cycle, doesn't actually accomplish anything other than keeping pundits in business.

The framework proposed in this book would go a long way to re-humanizing our elected officials. It would give them the capacity to be wrong, to recognize and respect the right of other people to have different opinions and to evolve their point of view to make more well-informed decisions and to actually compromise. It worked once when we formed the Constitution of the United States; it can work again.

WHAT THIS SYSTEM IS, AND WHAT IT'S NOT

With respect to our current government, we are operating under a system that is more than 225 years old. Over the years, the system has been modified and adapted. Sometimes the changes have been good (civil rights) and sometimes they've been bad (our absurd tax code). Of late, policy seems so much more often in the 'bad ' category than the 'good' one.

I have shared the central theme of this book – the balancing of political power across party lines to create a moderate and balanced government, and making the access to power stable and predictable – to many people whose opinions I deeply respect. It would be entirely too self-serving to say that those with whom I discuss my reforms generally support the idea. What's more meaningful is the common questions and objections I get. Every time I talk through this proposal with people, I learn more about what will make it effective. Questions and criticisms are an important part of making any idea or set of ideas better. This is certainly no exception. Accordingly, I have outlined some of the common questions and concerns I hear in talking this framework through. This is not an exhaustive list, but hopefully will clarify the logic behind this framework.

Question: This is all well and good, but I want to make sure I do not always have to choose between one party and the other. Doesn't this system too deeply institutionalize the party system?

Response: This is the most common piece of feedback I get when describing this framework. This makes total sense. Many people point to the party system as the root cause of the breakdown of Washington, D.C. as an effective set of institutions and worry that by so fully embracing the system, the problems of that system will only become further entrenched. To this, I would contend two things.

The first is that no matter how much people enjoy the romantic fiction of voter independence, when they're standing in that booth, the muscle memory of voting for that (R) or (D) candidate usually takes over. In other words, we're not nearly as independent as we like to pretend. We have to make the choice sets from which people are already choosing that much better. Embracing the party system as the solution to bringing balance back to governance doesn't undermine anyone's ability to vote according to preference. The difference is that once in effect, this system will move all candidates closer to the center, and thus have them be more representative of the views of the entire populace.

The second is the real argument that underlines the entire theory of this framework. By so radically embracing the party system, you rob it of its meaning. This system, in essence, calls the bluff of the professional rhetoricians. The sad reality is that many elected officials make quite a nice career out of doing little more than criticizing the opposition. By drawing things in such 'you're either with more or against me' terms, these politicians manage to rally people to a banner in moral terms that have nothing to do with effective governance. Bringing everyone back to the center, and completely embracing the party system as the way to do it, will have the net effect of neutering – or at least substantively undermining – the importance of the parties themselves. Or, to carry the statistic metaphor mentioned early forward, the net effect of this program is to actually create a shadow third party: the moderate party. We could call it the Mild Old Party, the MOP. As the system now represents citizens based on where they agree as opposed to where they don't, the (D) and (R) next to the names of the candidates matter so much less than what the actual names stand for.

Question: Can independent or third-party candidates still run for office?

Response: This is a tricky question to answer because it depends on which office such a candidate would be seeking. For the nation's highest elected office – the Vice Presidency – there should be no third-party candidates. Or more specifically, there could be no candidates who leave either party and run a campaign with the backing of their former party. The party committees can only support one candidate at a time.

The whole purpose of this system is to ensure that all parties have equal access to political power and that such power is predictable and stable. Removing the ambiguity of when a party will be in office and for how long they will hold an office is critical. With the path clear, the need for constant electioneering and campaigning plummets. Introduction of a third-party into the President-in-waiting election cycle could undermine the stability of this system. If third-party candidates were eligible to run for this office with the support of one of the two major parties, it could create a 'back-door' through which both parties could attempt to hijack the system and gain access to the executive function of government for longer than their allotted time. Whether they could succeed is beside the point. The very attempt to do so could undermine the spirit of the system and the effort would itself be profoundly disruptive.

That said, Americans will always have the freedom to vote for whoever they choose. The mechanism that filters an actual third-party candidate from a shill for one of the major parties is the support of the national committees. These committees, the Republican National Committee and the Democratic National Committee cannot offer support, financing, resources, etc. to any candidate when it's not their 'turn' to have a member of their party be elected Vice President. This is strictly a parameter on the national parties, and not on the American voter. If a viable third-party or independent gains support on their own merit, that would be fine.

While I highly doubt an Independent or any third-party could win the nation's highest elected office, especially given the limitations described above, such a scenario would present no disruption whatsoever. Should such a scenario arise in the election of the Vice President, the system would simply restore itself after the Vice President ascends to the Presidency. Upon this ascension, the next Vice Presidential candidate would simply be drawn from the party opposite of that of the outgoing President. House leadership would likewise be distributed 50/50 across both major parties. The Speaker of the House would be co-led position, with the role and responsibilities split by the Congressional heads of each party.

For other offices, the election of third-party or independent candidates is less important. As majority no longer determines leadership, the party affiliation matters less. From a House of Representatives perspective, third-parties would represent no change whatsoever to this framework. In terms of the Senate, should a third-party candidate come into office, the only significant impact would be to alter the 50/50 balance of the parties. As committee leadership will still be split evenly among the Democrats and Republicans, this aspect of governance would not be disrupted. The only change would come in terms of voting. Should Senators vote strictly on party lines, one party would now have a majority, as opposed to a perpetual 'tie.' If anything, this

HOW TO FIX AMERICA

only accelerates the need for compromise. What's more, with the rest of the reforms of this framework in place, the Senators themselves will be more moderate, reasonable and centrist. The majority in the Senate would mean much less than it does now. But to any extent that losing the 50/50 balance in the Senate would have impact, it would be mitigated by the balance in the House and in the Executive Branch.

Question: What happens if a President or Vice President dies in office, is impeached or resigns?

Response: If a President is unable to complete their term for any reason, the fix is simple. The Vice President simply ascends to the Presidency and the rest of the transition of power steps takes place accordingly. The American public then elects the next Vice President in a special general election. When the whole system is balance, it can absorb such extraordinary events much more easily.

Should a Vice President be unable to complete their term, their successor to the position will be elected by the American public in a special general election. No changes to the rest of the system need to be made. This Vice President would serve the balance of the President's term in office, and then follow the normal course through the transition of leadership.

As an extension of this line of thought, the probability of a President, or any other elected official, being impeached is extraordinarily low. But it's not unthinkable, and the very idea seems to have permeated the American consciousness. Ever since President Clinton was impeached by the House of Representatives, the language of impeachment is used by pundits and party extremists with increasing frequency. Do a quick search on the terms 'Impeach Bush,' or 'Impeach Obama.' You will be amazed at the language people use and the conviction in the belief that these men are evil, vile and corrupt and by extension, so too are their supporters. This type of language does nothing but entrench the acrimony in the system. It accomplishes nothing productive and brings out the worst in our elected officials. This framework will reverse this ugly trend and help us see the positives in those with whom we disagree.

Question: Couldn't politicians just keep switching parties?

Response: The only office for which this would be an issue would be in electing the Vice President, which is addressed above. Since the leadership in both houses of Congress is not determined by majority, such party switching doesn't really matter. In fact, it could be viewed as a sign of the health of the system. If a candidate is centrist enough that they could credibly switch parties – good for them and good for us. This framework will go a long way to filtering out political opportunists – people who only want office to hold it for its own sake.

Question: Does the system skew too much power to the opposition party?

Response: The Presidency is by far the most powerful political position in the American government. Nothing about this framework changes the importance of the Presidency. This power is heavily counter-weighted by the presence of an opposition President-in-waiting, an opposition House of Representatives and a Senate that will no longer be defined simply by party distribution.

In theory, if the Senate was evenly 50/50 across both parties, and Senators made a habit out of only voting on the party lines, the Vice President would have a lot of ties to break. This only makes the President and Vice President work more closely together, and sets the tone for how this relationship is managed at the transition in power.

The spirit of this system is to provide balance, and it accounts for the outsized power of the Presidency. It does not, however, give too much power to either side. It simply realizes the founding intention of our government to have a true system of checks and balances, which was the idea when our Founders put this whole thing together. We don't have balance. We do have separation of powers, but the powers are not applied to governance and reasonable policy.

Question: What will it take to enact true reform to the governance of the American system?

Response: The problem is not awareness. Most Americans would tell you that we are in the wrong place and heading in the wrong direction and that we are not being led by our elected officials. These politicians and the system in which they operate are as much the root cause of the challenges facing America as anything else. Most Americans have an intrinsic understanding of the problem.

What it will take is actual civility. Reform itself must be a moderate initiative. If enacted reforms are too extremist, on one side of the aisle or the other, such reforms will add to the further divide and exacerbate the problem. Everyone – citizens and politicians alike – are going to have to give up on being right and having all the answers. We can all start by setting the right tone and eliminating divisive political language from our own vocabularies. Going one step further, confront extremist positions – not to 'expose' them as wrong, but to remind people that no one side owns right or wrong absolutely.

As Ghandi so wonderfully said: "If we could change ourselves, the tendencies in the world would also change. As a man changes his own nature, so does the attitude of the world change towards him. We need not wait to see what others do." I can't think of a better way to describe our responsibility to each other and to ourselves.

Question: Will elected officials ever willingly up power?

Response: The answer to this is, sadly, probably not. Those in power have a vested interest in staying in power. While the method of administering government doesn't seem to be working for the American people, it sure does seem to be working for the politicians. They keep getting re-elected, and all they have to do is become full-time fund-raisers, and convince us that everyone who disagrees with them is evil. It's a pretty sweet gig, really. Of course, this is a dramatic oversimplification, but the point remains. Elected officials worry more about the 'elected' part than the 'official' part. And this is why they will never willingly enact a sweeping policy shift that limits their own power. It is obvious that politicians are more interested in power than governance. So, does this mean we are stuck with our system forever? Our system is going from bad to worse, and we keep more or less reelecting the same people into office, over and over.

There is no way that Washington, D.C. will reform itself under our current system. We need to modify, not destroy, the American system of governance. After all, there is so much that makes this a great country. For all its warts, I believe America to be the best nation in the world. At some point the American people must unite and lead Washington to do the same. Power must be removed from those that currently hold it. Power must be only granted to those that understand the nature of the trusted relationship between elected officials and their constituency. This particular framework will never get off the ground without a political sponsor and the backing of the votes of the American people.

WHAT NOW?

This is one idea on how we can approach change – true, genuine change – in our political order. But it is not the only idea. There are lots of great programs and reforms out there. In trying to stay true to the spirit of this book, nothing would make me happier than a civilized, moderate conversation about what is and what is not working in our government, where all ideas are welcome, and no one is cast aside. The longer we wait to reform our government, the more difficult the process of change will be once it reaches the point of inevitability.

If we can all agree that we need change, then it's time to get started. Let's have the conversations about what our true problems are and what solutions can address them. Let's listen to each other and understand each other.

Let's get to work.

About the Author

Phillip Barlag is an American citizen. He has spent his career in the private sector, most recently working in corporate sustainability. He is lives in the Atlanta, Georgia area with his wife and three children.

He would love to hear from you at phillipbarlag@gmail.com.

Thanks and Acknowledgements

I am incredibly grateful to so many people for all of their support, encouragement and guidance. I must first and foremost thank my wife Erin, whose love and belief in me certainly exceeds what anyone could ever hope to have. To my parents, Bruce and Kathy who still think I could grow up to be President. To my sisters, Katie and Amy, and their husbands, Brian and Chuck, who all enrich my life so much. To Pat and Jim Cain who – for some unknown reason – allowed me to marry their daughter and continue to be generous with their love and support.

Special thanks to Marc Mathieu who has been a great friend and mentor. Thanks to Laura Seydel, who more than anyone else, encouraged me to write this book. Thank you to those special people who are trying to help make the world a better place now and in the future, Steve Kline, Charlene Lake, Alex Lifttman, Pamela Miller, Ross Nicholson, Dailah Nihot, Judah Schiller, Kathrin Winkler, Anthony Zolezzi, and all the people trying to transform the way we think about the way the world works.

Made in the USA
Charleston, SC
26 September 2012